DEDICATION

*For Tom Herbst OFM
always encouraging and
stimulating*

*and
Abbot Jerome Hodkinson
an old friend
and valued critic*

ACKNOWLEDGEMENTS

*My gratitude to
Billy Collins,
former US Poet Laureate
for inspiring me with new vitality
and a fresh voice of my own;
also for kindly agreeing
to let me adapt the title of this book
from one of his.*

*John Wilkinson,
for his exuberant illustrations,
with hardly any interference from me.*

*Sister Wendy Beckett,
lover of art both visual and verbal,
for agreeing to write the Introduction.*

Mother Nikola and my Benedictine Sisters
for the opportunity to get this book together.

*Monica,
for lots of her time, and expertise.*

CONTENTS

INTRODUCTION 1
by Sister Wendy Beckett

PROLOGUE 3

SECTION 1
Aleph 6
The trouble about not writing poetry 7
Mind-Hoard 9
For Peter Levi 10
Constant moon 11
Fingering through the folds of our memories 12
Out beyond the playground 13
Manners 14
Green Song 15
Birthday 16
A question of Lifestyle 17
Persons 18
Encounter 19

SECTION 2
Vale of the White Horse 22
Meeting the unexpected in the bluebell wood 23
Holy Ghost 24
Sounds of autumn shades 26
Season for a song 27
Grief 28
So many silences 29
Ice-fishing 30

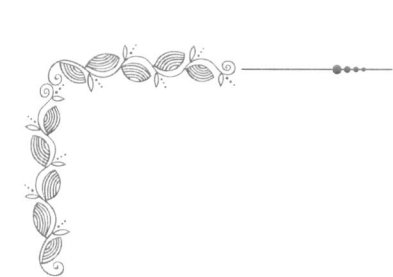

SECTION 3

Mathematics 34
Loss and Gain 35
Finding summer 36
For Ann 37
Getting on quite nicely thanks 38
Apple children 39
November 40
The little man in his signal-box 41
James comes 43
Silence 44
Silence; another way of putting it 45
At the window 46
Wind on a moonlit night 47

SECTION 4

Mary in the waiting wood 50
Mary's song 51
O that you would tear the heavens open and come down 52
Fiat 53
Shepherd's Tale 54
Silences 56
Jubilate 58
Threefold light 59
Ite ad Joseph 60
Cry for Syria 61

SECTION 5
I almost saw you   64
Issues   65
Sun's captive   67
The Door   68
Storming Heaven   69

SONNETS
Beauty Risen   72
Lachrymae Rerum   73
Terra Incognita   74
Sonnet for Jean Leclercq   75
On "The Mother with the sleeping Child"   77
On hearing Bach's B Minor Prelude and Fugue   78
Trinity   79
Pietà   81

EPILOGUE
Part 1   85
Part 2   89

INTRODUCTION
by Sister Wendy Beckett

Poetry is a mysterious business. Perhaps we all have poetry within us – silently, inarticulately. Since we cannot find the words, our poetry dies unheard, even by ourselves.

Because poetry is essentially words, we see, we delight, we wonder, we grieve, we despair: but only words, the true words, perfect, exactly fitting, can make explicit, either to ourselves or to others, these emotions or thoughts. But poetry is more than finding the precise and evocative word: these words must be not only clear, but musical, singing together with the words on either side if they are to transmute our formless feelings, our intuitions and convictions, into poetry.

Words then, but words made musical. By themselves words are prose, that fine thing. It is their arrangement in a profound sequence, where each word means more in the arrangement than it does in isolation, that creates what we call poetry.

This gift, rare and wonderful, has been given to Sister Mary Stephen. Words in their most blessed order are where she finds a truth otherwise inexpressible. Then sights and sounds, the desires and the feelings that are personal to her become luminous for everybody. She enables that right, true, witty and luminous word to make a

leap across the threshold of longing into
the bright field of encounter.

Most beautifully and precisely she can tell us:

To feel is real enough
but flint must spark off stone.
word is the rock I crave
for what I name is known.

The whole world is flint to Sr Mary Stephen.

PROLOGUE

Here is a pot-pourri of poems; both of the heavenly and of the more mundane. Any poem has a unique personality, yet relates to something beyond the personal, and if these poems speak of things beyond your or my understanding, at least they might lead us to see a break in the "cloud of unknowing." The lighter poems indicate my firm belief in God's having a wonderful sense of humour.

Some of the poems need to be delivered in their particular regional accent. For example "Shepherd's Tale" has to be recited with a Northern accent, which means that it lends itself to a more informal dialogue in Mystery Play genre. "Issues" has to be rendered in a Kentish accent, for the fun of it. Some poems were born with Received Pronunciation, which no longer exists, but the poems are indifferent to this; they are adaptable. Some were born fifty years ago; some more recent models reflect "the very laughter of God," if one were to be so bold, and why not! All flows to and from Him. The finger of God creating Adam was in touch with his creation, and will continue to be, everlastingly.

I think I ought to throw some light on the title of this collection; it explains where some of the poems come from. I cannot break the seal of the Confessional, since I happen to have been the penitent. I was feeling confused about the question of spending time writing poetry in relation to my vocation as a contemplative nun. The priest to whom I mentioned this reminded me of the gifts we are to employ in the service of our Maker and told me that as a penance I was to write a poem. I obeyed and called it "The Trouble about Not Writing Poetry." I had just read Billy Collins' book of poems, "The Trouble with Poetry," so the idea of the title sprang to mind, although his message was different. Billy Collins does not know why I wanted to adapt his title but he graciously allowed me to do so. The fact of the matter is that poetry will out. It needs to get out of the house; to make friends.

SECTION 1

Aleph

Aleph, one humble and wise, there before the sound,
waiting for that split mini–second, and inhaling
a feather breath, allowing the beginning
of the birth of a word.
Beth, the exhaling of Creation, but Aleph, quiet
there before, in the wings with the Holy Dove
hovering over the world's waters.
She dwelt in awe inside the vast reaches
of the Father's silence, as he had
inhaled and exhaled the WORD, in the beginning.
And now she sits silently beside me, inside me
in prayer, as I inhale, listen to, absorb the silence
between the Father and the Son;
a shared quietness, enabling the outbreathing
of the Holy Ghost with all gifts
and fruits for the taking.

The trouble about not writing poetry

The trouble about not writing poetry is a matter
for monkeys, who evolved the strategy.
First, you must cover your eyes in case you happen to notice
those blue, double cornflowers outside the window
of the room where you have breakfast.
Just don't watch as they struggle out of their
black velvet laced bodices, enticingly it has to be said,
even on a cold June morning.

Plus, you have to be careful to avoid the stare of
a tall, elegant escholtzia clearly reprimanding you
(with more than a touch of hauteur) for looking
and daring to address her by the common name
of Californian Poppy. Take refuge from
her stare; keep your head down, as you warm
your hands round a mug of coffee.

Please don't look through your fingers, breaking the rules
just to see a cheeky blackbird, hands behind his back
thrusting into the shrubbery for a quick snack,
and certainly custody of the eyes is essential or
you might notice that each blade of grass is standing
to attention: green and diamond uniform emblazoned
with his Maker's monogram.

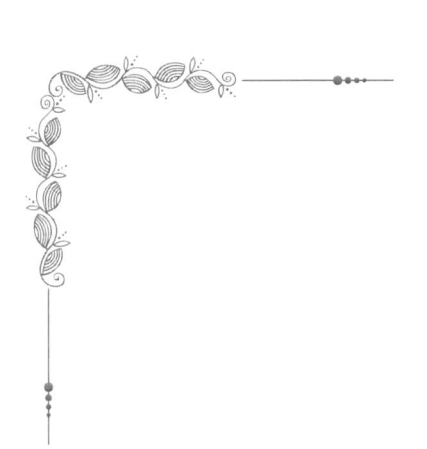

Ears at the muffle, in case you are overcome with marvel
at the blackbird or chaffinch playing 'catch me' with
their to and fro, the thrill of tuning up before
a rapturous dawn chorus. You wouldn't be listening anyway to
the magpie (way out of tune), but you can't miss the
screaming seagull, wings outspread like a small boy playing
aeroplanes: both are dangerous!

Better to deal with beauty with no words, and while you are
working that out, don't even think of writing a poem
about it; just toss all ideas, unusual facts,
interesting conversations into an old sea-chest:
climb in with them, bang down the lid against
invaders; press SHUT DOWN and go to the place where
neither rust nor moth consume.

Mind–Hoard

Shall the fabric
of my mind,
woven with care
on my heart's loom
depict another man's design?

Shall my thread
of fine gold
reeled in the quiet
of my own room
spin secret tales already told?

Or, shall the work
of my own hand
seen in a glimpse
through a half-open door
share some part of my heart's land?

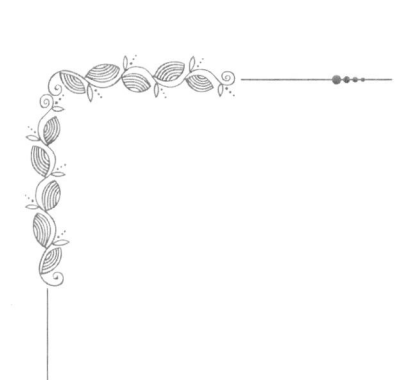

For Peter Levi

You have not fixed in me
this flint articulate.
It meets your steel and see
I reason and create.

My mind's a wick so dead,
I quite forgot its flames.
You teach and fresh things said
revive my embered dreams.

You did dissect my mind
with fire rational as ice.
Precision of intent
quickens my paralysis.

To feel is real enough
but flint must spark off stone.
word is the rock I crave
for what I name is known.

Constant moon

Is not a lover wise to court the moon,
whose sickle measures time, who isolates
the fruit tree in the shadow she creates,
full-blown her icy bloom, who wanes alone?
Foolhardy it would be to trust the sun,
deceiving those he floods and permeates,
absorbing with the fire he generates
crying 'You cease to be, for we are one'.

Yet even in the general, wholesome sun
his touch can halt the ruthless hand of time
leaves carved in relief of green and startling lime
embossed in the blue of a lost afternoon.
and round the still, red apple the bright bird's lone
song rings a sudden, personal chime,
snatched jealously back to the beat of prime
note and matchless fruit, which blend as one.

How constant, true and maiden is the moon!
If isolate, aloof from sanity
men mock her madness as inconstancy
they are day's fools for, raving the sun;
in masquerade the sage is a buffoon.
The orchard trees assume identity;
they truly are in separate mystery,
their own shade cast by the rational moon.

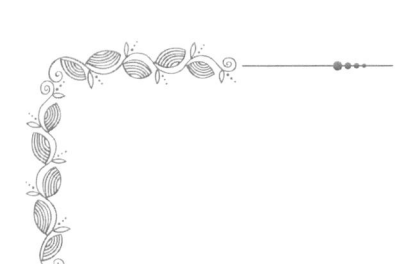

Fingering through the folds of our memories

Can't count the times I've leaned on that gate
at the end of the lane just past the copse
where the trickle of a stream paddles under
branches in the dense, nearly-green
of an early Spring.

I'd always stop, just to lean into the spinney; to
breathe in the earthy smell,
and I'd get that ache of nostalgia
pulsing through the acoustic of birdsong
of an early morning.

Of course, it took me longer to reach the gate
unable to curb this window-gazing;
such display of the season's sales to allure;
dressing-up, posturing of the trees in glamour;
'Coming out' - young things!

We've seen it all before, spring upon spring.
What seasons' fashions we gloat over;
offers we never bargained for,
as we finger through the folds
of our memories.

Out beyond the playground

I sit down to write,
and I'm wondering where this poem is
before it hits the page; before I grab a
pen, collar the notion and press it
into service.

Today it's in the playground
where letters are at their games,
dancing in a ring; making up rules
for grown-ups to follow.

"Come on" they shout, as off they go
through the creaky gate of rote and ABC
into the wonderland of best friends and tales;
devouring "Dandy" and "Beano."

They run home helter-skelter, longing for
the blissful smell of the weekly comic they find
on the doormat, and maybe it will be
the smell of new bread too.

You stumble into a poem often on the
heels of wonder, over the doorstep
of things you've forgotten you remembered
and always it takes you by surprise
like a catch in the slips.

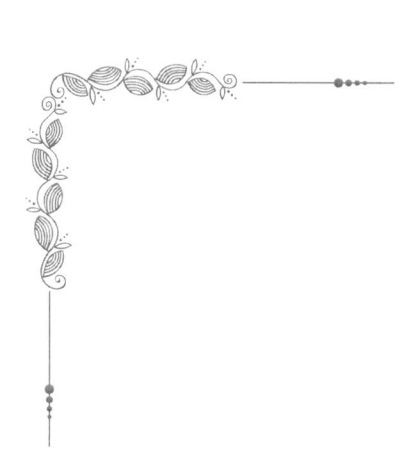

Manners

If a word is someone,
and has friends,
consider how determine
whom he meets
and where he stands.

There may be many
times when he
will thank you for observing
customs old
and courtesy.

Green Song

I thought it was March today;
clean with new green, just winter wheat.
There was mud and blue sky in the puddles;
March sounded as two birdnotes sweet.
The bird did not feel the end of things;
he felt birth not death in the sky.
Quiet, we wait the thrush and I.
March, remember we sang for you
in December.

It will be March one day;
there'll be new green leaf and grass.
Though it grow into April and May
March will capture me nor let me pass.
In case I make a mistake again,
I will find a quiet place for my heart;
set it carefully in the dark.
How it will come into flower for you
in a March shower.

Birthday

We all speculate about the way
God used his might to say
'Let there be light'.
We may side with those who
follow the biblical narration
explicitly,
or we may peel our bananas
with nostalgia
and enjoy our tea parties,
though observers annoy us.
God really must find it odd
that we chatter on
about matter.
In fact, it's immaterial how.
I maintain we should not allow
Creation to become
a hypothetical situation.
We are only too conscious of
some kind of fall
and jubilant Resurrection.
The main thing: there was a birth
of the earth.
Once upon a time
there was none.
Then it began. Man
was new. So were you.

A question of Lifestyle

It was one of those questions
going the rounds when I was young:
Would you like to have your life woven
in red and gold, or blue and silver?
I agonised about it and I nearly said
"I choose both" but I wasn't too sure
about that holy option.
Now I'm old I know how right
it would have been.
All or nothing.

I mean, to lie on my back under a clear
blue sky in a field uninhabited by
sheep, cows or livestock of any
denomination, and the grass has to be dry,
hot, a silver stream close by
discreetly murmuring and, by the way
an absolutely mosquito-free zone;
this is my blue and silver,
top-level experience.

It may of course be a matter of mood,
or perhaps a well-rounded and
full-blooded split personality.
I worry about it. You see, there are days
when I would prefer to stride out amongst
the crowds, preceded by heralds in red tabards
blowing bright trumpets, and followed by ladies'
maids brushing my golden tresses. Yet on a
blue and silver day I've been known to leap up
bouleversée, on glimpsing a field of buttercups
through a gap in the hedge.

Persons

The Father, creative,
economical with words;
prodigal as to works.
Word spoken: a new thing is.
"Let there be… and it was."

The Son, the Word
forth from the Father's mouth;
reveals the unimaginable,
Jesus walks the world over.
Whoever sees me, sees the Father.

And the Holy Ghost, the Lover
inspiring, dancing, darting
between One and Other
encircling devouring Fire;
indescribably Gifted.

Encounter

You catch a glimpse of Him peering through the lattice,
but once through the doorway of surrender
you see Him clearly, leaping over the mountains,
bounding over the hills,
running to meet you.

So leave the life-long dance
through mansions, over islands,
scanning the far horizon for a shadow
even when you have known
in the darkness, His desire.

Must it be slowly, carefully? No! Tear open
eagerly the invitation of the Word
He let fall beneath the casement, and
leap across the threshold of longing into
the bright field of encounter.

You saw Him, as I told you earlier,
running to meet you, lithe with grace.
Did I remember to tell you, though, how
He was ablaze with the fire of delight,
exultant at the final encounter?

You'll find yourself saying what you were taught
with no hesitation: O that He would kiss me
with the kisses of His mouth!
More, much more, than you were given
to know before, while watching
and searching on the journey.

SECTION 2

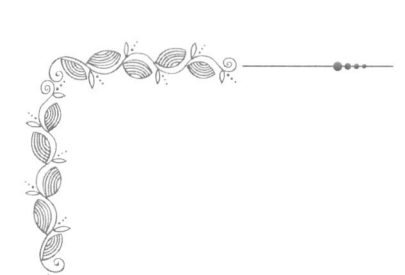

Vale of the White Horse

Wild wind rode the horse-cloud
hard upon the hill.
Fled before him
the young-year sun,
running headlong the field over.
Shadow before and after, but now
is sunlight. Follow there!
There, where the wind scoops the sun
out of a bowl in the hill
to spill it all in the valley.
Here, now quick, follow,
as swallow swooping low
to brush the washed grass
shining green to see it pass.
Pale, quicksilver sun,
can I capture you, are you won
by a fleeting reflection seen
in my heart?
Or must I wait
till late, gold sunlight
focus into strength?

Meeting the unexpected in the bluebell wood

About fifty-five years ago to the day,
out walking in the bluebell woods
with a friend, we saw something so startling;
quite out of the ordinary really,
I can't resist revisiting it, and by the way
should you wish to check it out,
there is yet time, as we are both still alive.

Out then together in this wood, we saw
in front of us, not more than six feet away,
poised on a wooden fence in broad daylight
scrutinizing us, bold as brass and solemn as
an old taxidermist, was a humongous,
Tawny Owl.

We approached cautiously, not allowing a twig
to snap underfoot, in case it should disappear
without leaving even a grin behind.
It moved nary a muscle.
We exchanged scrutinies without a word,
and deciding tacitly on a slight bow,
we walked on.

Well, you have to admit that a modicum
of astonishment is in order, on chancing upon
unusual events. We have to be open to anything,
I thought as I strode across the yard, unlocked the car and
sliding in, found the Holy Ghost in the passenger seat
smiling as He carefully fastened His seat belt.

Holy Ghost

It just seemed like any other day;
a high day, a holiday it turned out.
I was sitting in stillness
as usual,
then, no preamble, it seemed there was
a partying balloon inside me; exciting
if rather
disconcerting.

What had it to do with
inner stillness, prayerful encounter?
Plenty of room actually
for the apophatic,
but this rising dough —
it was not unlike bread in the making —
was making merry
within me.

What was to be done
about this masked jester; an uninvited guest
entering without the common courtesy
of knocking?
Well, as usual, the Two were there,
passing the silence to and fro between them
giving nothing away, that is nothing
very practical.

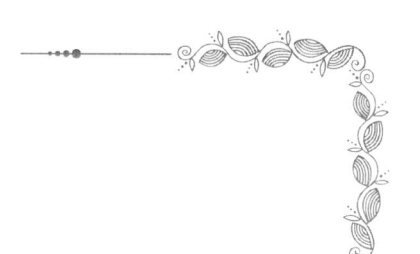

Should I give up; surrender
to this masquerading stranger invading
my space; entertain this buffoon;
give in to such light-headedness;
these bursts of smothered laughter?
I ought at least to have some means,
of identification.

Well! As if I hadn't recognised you,
at it again, Holy Ghost,
wild Card, always played to win the trick
unexpectedly: completing the threefold gift,
providing for a lifetime of unwrapping.
Joy — layer upon layer — here, there, forever
with basketsful of fragments
for sharing.

Sounds of autumn shades

A viola should bow
such strata of sunset;
sustain copper sun,
note vibrant and low;
key to golden and let
silence linger it yet.

Or scherzo the green,
trees in the grey wind.
Leaves pizzicato,
dance in round, keen
cast eager behind
boughs no power to bind.

Rust robin does try.
Wire stave for his music,
quaver and rest,
Come bluetit slate high;
grate black crow and creak,
background his lyric.

Who chords then the colours?
Can random scales shade, crowned,
mount to last movement
reach summit? Adore!
Silver triad resound,
in one Lord of bright sound

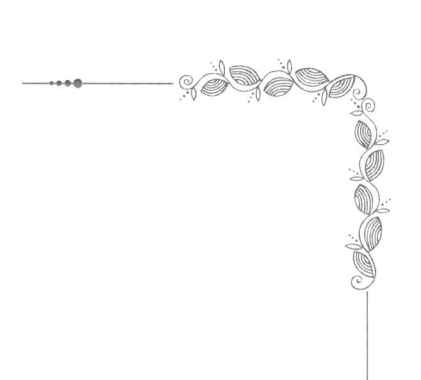

Season for a Song

Thin note spins robin;
autumn's come in.
Hear arrogant fellow,
"Match me with yellow
leaves."
Grieves not for summer:
song's over

Grief

"Ron is dead; and it was in a half-hour."
Ethel said, when she could tell it
on the phone
without crying through it.

She said, "He used to say every
night, 'Good night, Fruit'
that's what he said, every night"
He always called her "Fruit."

Ethel said "I love you very much Ron"
Every night they both said that.
It was sudden. She said, "I'll help you
Ron, I'll clean up, no trouble."

But he died. The worst thing was when
next day she found his budgie
dead too. "Of a broken heart" we told
her on the phone when she rang.

Mornings, Ron said "Good morning;"
Budgie would say "Good morning."
Of a night Ron said "Nightie-night sleep well;"
Budgie did too, perched on Ron's sausage finger.

"Never mind, Mum," said the daughter
"he's with Dad now." And
"when it's all over…"
Ethel keeps saying between tears.
"when it's all over, I'll get
another budgie."

So many silences

The silence, as you stop
on a dark night, coming home
through the lonely alley,
listening for a footfall behind you.

The silence of the missed heartbeat,
when the child listens for a key to
turn in the lock as the last bus stops
with her Mum and Dad on it?

Silence in the darkness of the bedroom;
Christmas dawn just before the child
remembers, and feels for the lumpy
stocking; begins to wish or guess.

The silence after deep snowfall;
between lightning and thunderclap;
first chirp and dawn chorus;
birth of the baby and the longed for cry.

The silence after the baton is tapped
and the instruments give tongue,
between the spark of an idea
and the poet's word.

The silence after the clock stops,
and the knob turns; before the
face appears round the door;
the silence after the gate clangs.

The silence after the lie,
before the knife thrust. Or,
let's lighten up! Silence before…
the prompt, the punchline, the applause!

Ice-fishing

I'll bet I was the only person
on the planet
who'd never heard the details of it
– yesterday –
I mean the time of the year when the man
slammed the door
and left.

Perhaps the woman was washing the dishes
at the time,
more likely, composing an email
to their daughter
on holiday
in Tenerife.

The cat washing scrupulously
behind an ear,
provocatively doing Pilates,
back paw stretched towards the table lamp,
his shadow like a
roasted turkey.

The woman wasn't listening
when the truck
belched into gear actually. She was
surfing the internet, googling
for her own personal
escape route.

The other men, shouting
and laughing as they stowed gear
into the back
and, wrapped tight in their thermals,
roared away down the
pitch black street.

You'll be thinking understandably,
that this is the sad story of a parting;
no drama, no memory
of a last word,
not even a curse
to cast after his departure.

But hang on in there! We were standing
by the Aga in the kitchen yesterday,
this Canadian
and I, when she came out
with this amazing,
exhilarating fact:

The truck will fetch up eventually
on the deepest ice of the northernmost lake;
the men will pitch camp,
light a fire,
drill a huge hole in the ice
and... FISH!

So will you join me please in being astonished?
We shall augment shoals of folk
who get excited by the unusual
and true facts
which surround us,
more gaping mouths opening for a bite.

SECTION 3

Mathematics

The oneness of One, I do proclaim,
merits our prime speculation.
Being before the beginning;
singing solo, but also
mirror dancing with One's image
Proclamation!

The twoness of Two, I do maintain
worthy of consideration:
mathematics never prosaic
discloses its soul.
Two becomes a Love affair;
Creation!

The threeness of Three I ascertain,
firelights a focus in family,
for childhood long upon a time
met its trinity in tale.
Bears – Mice – Pigs –
Perfection!

So, counting on is endless,
as happy numbers herd
towards Infinity
similar and motley
to converge in Final
Resolution!

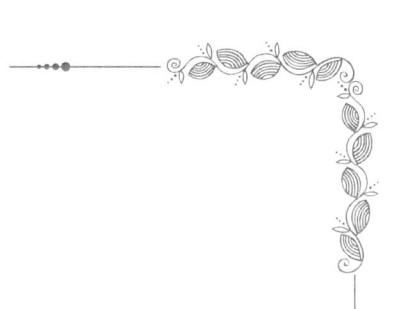

Loss and Gain

What, falter at the failure of our Spring;
has it not cost us everything?
How else should loss amount to more
than yet we have accounted for.

I call to mind what life and love invest
in small green births and all the rest,
but when no profits shall accrue
must we not be Spring's debtors too?

The muted bluebells did not wake this wood
for horns of gold all secret stood.
These singing flowers that make us wait
will sing though it might be too late.

So I advise you how to deal with pain.
Depreciate and count as gain
the time-devalued Spring, and tears
our fixèd assets of the years.

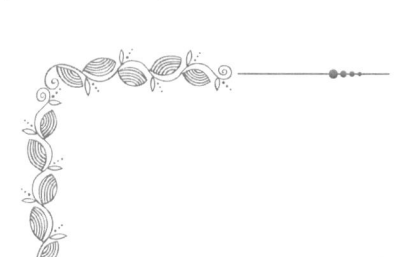

Finding summer

I'll tell how instantly I discovered
all summer in the tall grass:
red ladybird climbs higher there;
wings hover.
Gone!
Meanders dilute a season
I care for.

Suppose I answer your glance, uncover
branches, ash, your tousled hair,
net a blue butterfly on the wing
better to ponder,
caught.
A look nearly captures a season
I care for.

Perhaps, when old, I shall recover
my startled blue child's gaze.
Maybe I shall wander then, savour,
wonder over;
saunter and linger, then handle
this squandered treasure; this season
I care for.

For Ann

Is it inconsequence
when, intense,
grey eyes cool,
Tom, no fool
says the moon
followed him to school?

If it mattered
a bird battered
his night-pane,
why, tell again
fear of owl hoots
in the lane.

Tom at three
can freshly see
the morning moon.
I would as soon
meet him now,
nor wait till noon.

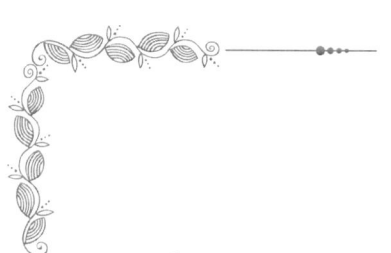

Getting on quite nicely, thanks

If I were you, and I'm sure
you are awfully glad I'm not,
I'd be in the seventh heaven
tomorrow when I woke up and knew
I was seventy-seven because seven, as you
know, being of a Biblical disposition,
is a Very Important number.
Should you be unaware of this fact
you might be overcome by rather glum
feelings about being seventy-seven.
But let's face it: the mere fact that
your feet and legs have worked out
the mechanics (in conjunction with your brain)
of carrying around the rest of you
fairly briskly for most of the last
seventy-five years is not bad going,
though I know when every knee should bend
yours does, now and again, refuse.
In conclusion: there is a great cause for rejoicing
in the admirable summation of reaching seventy-seven
and continuing to be in, more or less, perpetual motion.
Meanwhile, I had this dream about standing on the edge
of a high cliff with a group containing nuns, who just stepped
delicately off and drifted down to the blue, blue sea – wonderful!
feet and legs not needed on voyage.

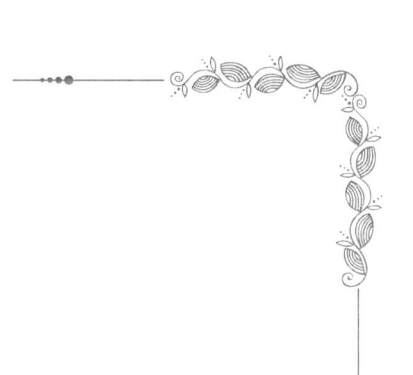

Apple children

Sun's up, orchard's awake, see
bonny mother apple tree
cuffs the leaves; chides the chucking bird,
her apple children can't be heard
but they smile when I come,
thumb in, every one.
When wicked winds creep round they'll be
indoors with me.
Comfort a-plenty.
Summer's in the pantry.

November

O the end of the year's in flames!
Red hedges burn berries:
leaves in cinders, fire is
embers underfoot.

Look, how my ash-bones frame
a blue cameo, the brash starling
silks and preens,
gossips overhead.

The sky pales too soon.
Gold threads through dead trees;
I am held quite
in last light.

O the year ends in fanfare;
heralds a new beginning.
There shall be no mourning
in our new life.

The little man in his signal-box

This morning without warning,
someone threw me a line and from the start
I should have taken a firm line,
but I had the bit between my teeth
as you would have, given
a similar kind of
punch-line.

I gnawed at it all day;
nearly went online to resource the word.
I didn't, because that would have been
the bottom line, though I have to admit
it was touch and go that I might do:
in fact it was almost
borderline.

No, I said sternly to myself,
draw the line: you can't do that.
Think it through; just work out
a storyline about, maybe, a little man
called Stan living near
the railway line in a signal box off
a lonely branch-line.

This rather retiring, mustachioed
sad, little man could perhaps have a job
on the side; a change, a
different line from work with
his trains; perhaps he had an artistic
streak and was proficient in line-drawing
line-dancing, even.

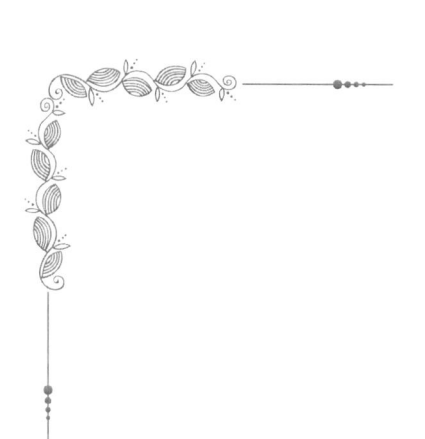

He certainly needed something
to raise his spirits; to give his life purpose,
to pinpoint the fine line between living simply
and simply living; also, he did need to apply
himself to his diminishing waistline,
for even a little man can't live for long below
the breadline.

Especially as he gets older and his hair-line
recedes, as do his teeth. Anyway, this man had
left the touchline decades ago, and now
he was nearing the finishing line.
He never made the headline;
he just had to toe the line
like all of us when the timeline is up: meet
the deadline.

James comes

James comes. He is eight and older;
he brings poems in a folder.
His heart breeds bolder
enterprise;
his eyes bright butterflies
his words wise.
Winters of wind bring confusion;
my blood needs transfusion.
Sometimes the old rhyme
or the odd rhyme
makes our thoughts chime
out of chasms of time.
In age is no difference;
we seek reassurance,
a presence.

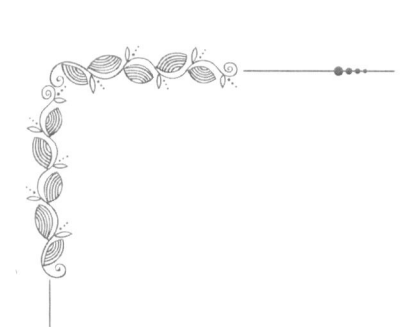

Silence

Silence is soil;
thrust roots in it.
Ploughman and toil
work life from it.

Delve below layers;
thoughts furrow it.
Quiet loams, and your
strong hand turns it.

Silence holds word,
mind-hoard treasures it;
ideas unheard
grow rich in it.

Down I sank, down
then I knew it.
Graft to the vine
bore fruit to it.

Silence; another way of putting it

I must tell you about the
silence of the soil,
and the toil of the ploughman
working life from it.

Quietly delving below the layers;
how he turns, furrows
and loams it
with a strong, sure hand.

The silence of his mind-hoard;
holding ideas and
words unheard;
growing richer with working.

The soil's silence is in him;
he is graft to stem
then, the shoot.
His love of the silence, his fruit.

At the window

I meet the sky
early and late.
The pupils of my heart
dilate.

There are no clouds
I sink and rise
cast into fathoms
of your eyes.

I dredge the air
sifting the blue.
Brave me, to bear
the want of you.

But star the sky
when night has come
so I shall know
you are at home.

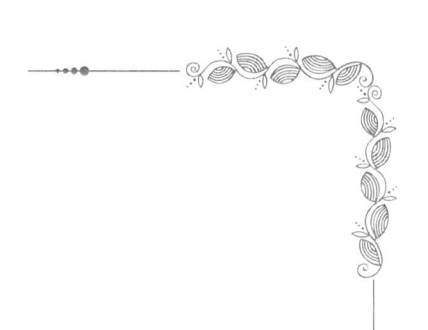

Wind on a moonlit night

Weather, O you are wild!
Finish with the leaves,
leave the tree, child!

Quiet, you are there mind,
crouching under night's
irritable wind.

Blustered into such sleep.
What proud moon-dreams
these wild nights keep.

SECTION 4

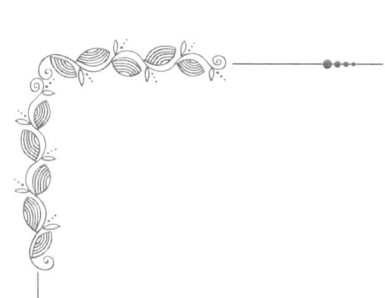

Mary in the waiting wood

Tree, tell me
how to be all still;
without stir, without breath,
naked, brown arms
strong outheld to the far sky;
hushed, hung, held
yet vibrant with pulsing Spring.

No sounds.
Silence rounds,
rings the tree. Tree,
can you hear me
straining the stillness;
my soul's silence lifted to
the limits of creation's response?

Tree, tell me
that we understand one another;
we share together
the warm life welling within us.
Shall I dwell with you in the waiting wood;
alone, a quiet maiden
becoming a mother?

Mary's Song

I woke, containing you, singing a new song.
Fire's element mastered in flame, fashions a form;
love's pulse within me shall be shaped a man, but
can spirit be birth-bound; merit a mother and warm?

White winter falls silent and cold;
we wait loving, and still I sing but more
turn in to my womb where silences eddy,
gyrate, and soundless break on an unseen shore.

Quick child within the dark, does know, sees,
hears; must never lose myriad wonder of flower-
colour, chromatics that counter and fuse, nor
rise out of reach moon and his bright star.

You win me earth's essence and warm.
Lunar beauty is bliss, and cannon in far skies
those singing stars I know may now be dust.
No matter: I saw my child in the angel's eyes.

Creation spirals, rounds, barely I touch
eternal its rim with quiet fingers. On tips
of silence that angel is poised beyond darkness,
yet I shall suckle at my mere breast his lips.

O, that you would tear the heavens open and come down

From where we stand, the Cave is dark.
We wait in this valley of darkness; this night
of shadows and echoes from the past.

The Father is aware, but silent;
the Watchers are there, mute and still;
the Holy Ghost broods with quiet joy.

Moses is there in a cleft of the rock;
Plato observes the images thrown on the wall
by the fire outside, near the sheep-fold.

In this silence and darkness is no threat,
for waiting there is right; without signs.
Mary has said her Fiat and it shall be.

The door pushed open by the shepherds,
casts another shadow on the wall;
image of a cross, for pain is there before birth.

Then, at the breath of a new Creation
uttered by the Father, the Holy Ghost stirs;
Jesus slips into the waiting world.

The Father tears open the curtains of heaven,
beside Himself with the weight of joy
at this first glimpse of His only Son,

Child, you shine at your birth, translucent
with love of the Father, who sees even now, how
the veil of the temple will be rent at your death.

Fiat

Mary said 'Fiat' and He was, in time;
flesh of her flesh
bone of her bone.
And the Infinite
was contained and grew.
And evening came and morning came
the First day.
Mary said 'Fiat Lux'
as she gave light: she brought forth.
And there was Light.
And evening came and morning came,
the fullness of time
the ninth month.
She smoothed his eyelids
and he opened his eyes
to meet her gaze.
She said simply:
"It is very good."
Is it right to put the words of God
on Mary's lips?
Well, the Word was in her heart,
Jesus the fruit of her womb.

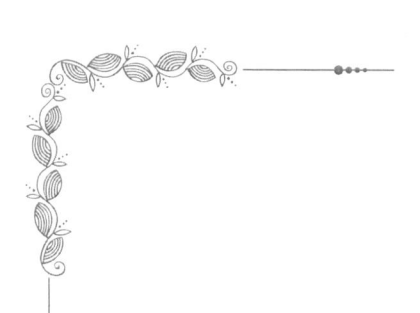

Shepherd's Tale

You wouldn't have cared for the night-shift, I can tell you,
not at the year's end,
with the wind
slashing your face and numbing your aching mind;
and the snow; the bitter reality of it
seeping through the traditional gear,
which was, to say the least, inadequate.
We had it to do, but I think you'd
back us up when we say we would have preferred
to stay at home, in bed with our warm wives,
and a good long sleep in front of us –
for choice.
You realise, I'm sure, that was before,
grumbling all together
in a huddle like the sheep;
before the instant of terror and the withering fear,
the shrapnel-shock, the streams of shell-light.
And when we dared to open our eyes to the skies' blinding,
suddenly shattered out of our found senses
exploded into another world,
hurled on our ears the singing, singing heavens.

We soon moved off though some cynics were ready
to think we'd misunderstood.
But I knew when they said manger that's what they meant.
We went down into the town.
The party-goers coming home late thought we'd gone mad;
perhaps we had, but by then, there wasn't a man
would have turned back.
You'll be wondering how we felt when we knelt there
so near the baby and that young Mary?
Hard for a poor chap like me to express it really.
The light and the singing were gone;
just a smelly stable and the animals munching away.
A bit of an anti-climax in a way.
But you see we knew who it was there, sharing his bed
with the beasts, and we appreciated
our poverty after that;
after God had spoken his own Word
in our language
uncouth and poor.

Silences

Listen to the silence between
the Father and the Word.
Withdraw with Mary
into the silence
of the womb.

Wonder in awe with
the silent Watchers.
But also, see and sing
with those Angels
at a simple birth.

Cover His little feet
with kisses, remembering
the tears and joy
of another Mary and
another time.

Touch His tiny fingers;
believe as Thomas, in
a wounded hand
holding for you
the Holy Bread.

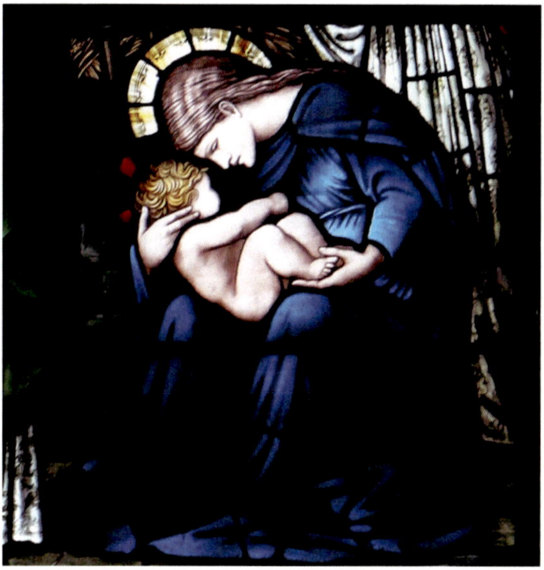

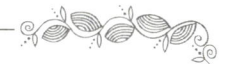

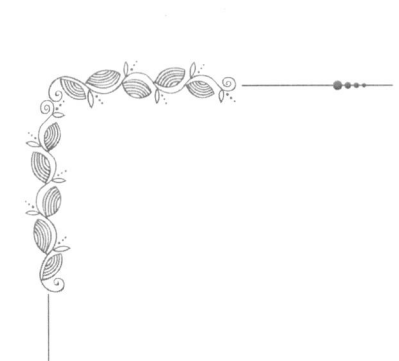

Jubilate

I need only the pin-point of an idea
for my angel to dance on,
and then my mind being a magnet,
zillions of angels hone in
and settle with folded wings
dove-tailing neatly and quietly;
white swans; a celestial snowdrift
massing on a sloped roof.

Then, once gathered, at my signal
they begin: pianissimo..piano
swelling to forte… fortissimo, wings open,
with unrestrained revel of harmony they
split the welkin with 'Gloria in excelsis,'
which is, after all what they are meant
to do in Heaven and sometimes on earth
in angelic and, actually, kataphatic fashion.

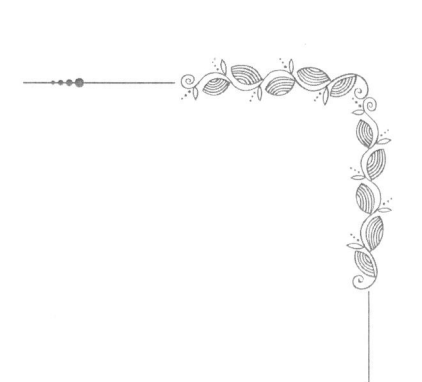

Threefold light

Quiet midnight:
Child in starlight
new-born lies.

Maid elected:
flame reflected
from her eyes.

Silence broken:
last Word spoken
God's first cries.

Ite ad Joseph

Then we come to Joseph, as bidden.
A word about him, another chosen one.
I should like to state quite firmly
that he would not have had the time
to stand about holding lilies,
dressed in a green and brown robe.
He was most probably not old and balding,
but definitely good and conscientious
at his job; great with lathe, saw and suchlike.
He loved Mary; the real Mary, before statues.
After all, he was betrothed to her;
they were preparing for life together.
And then this sudden inconceivable 'I've something
to tell you' and the fuller version to himself from
an Angel, no less. Joseph must have been shattered,
together with all his plans for the future, into a turmoil of
confusion; maybe angry even at first.
Mary seemed so sure; sticking to her story: 'An Angel spoke to me;
gave me a request from God'. How could she not say 'Yes'?
She even managed to be serene and absolutely certain.
But a baby! To make sense of that – How?
Only through Mary's steady love of him; her evident purity,
her innocence. She became his rock to cling to, but he was her
anchor; her protector in danger; faithful husband
and a loving father to the Father's only Son.

Cry for Syria

Let us pray,
but please don't
use your Church voice
so neat and tidy;
crisp and Sunday clean;
sanitised, anaesthetized.
SCREAM!!!
even if it shocks.
That young boy with half his face
blown off. He screamed
and screamed; they heard him in Syria;
they must have heard him in Heaven.
Jesus!
this was your homeland;
YOU WERE BORN NOT THAT FAR AWAY
YOU CAN MAKE IT ALL END.
Silent night, Holy night
All is calm...
So many places where the little kids
don't know calm; never had the chance to listen to silence,
only waited and watched their mother's anxious eyes;
waited for the next burst of gunfire;
the next bomb.
Some places, the bigger kids learn how to kill –
they teach them how to kill;
double murder of innocents.
small persons without names – and then without limbs;
little people, unknown to us
in reasonably peaceful places.
Christmas Child, you are too tiny for Calvary.
They were there before you and after,
trying to learn how not to be afraid.
Let there be peace on earth – Soon, Soon!!
Amen.

SECTION 5

I almost saw you

It was your finger putting the finishing touches
to the world's edge of the downs today
wasn't it?
Just smoothing off, satisfied, pleased
with that perfect, bold brush-stroke;
not another touch until
man comes, on this great white horse.
I almost saw your hand, as I turned aside
didn't I?
A tear-prick away from nearly
catching you at creation today;
unaware you were,
observing your own bright shadow.

It was the sliver-glimpse of you slipping through
the wildflower meadow beyond the field today
wasn't it?
Not quite hidden, bending down to cornflower
poppy and daisy, tracing their petals
as a mother contours her child's face.
You nearly caught my eye as I turned
didn't you?
Just a moth-wing away from nearly catching you
at creation today.
But did you know that I heard, well almost,
the swish of the hem of your garment
as you passed by that day?

Issues

Now, she goes,
I'd like to explain about this new phase
in his ongoing therapy, right?
Ah, I thought, warily does it.
Try to know without knowing,
if you get my meaning.

You see, she went on,
It isn't easy. I do try
really I try, but I don't think
I listen to him – know what I mean?
Yes, I think so, I said.

I think he's trying to tell me something;
something Big like, get it?
He's wanting me to listen to him;
at a deep level,
you know?

Ah! I said, you have a gut reaction
that we are dealing with Issues
at this moment in time?
Ooh! she goes, I'm so grateful
to meet with someone so understanding.
Thank you for that.

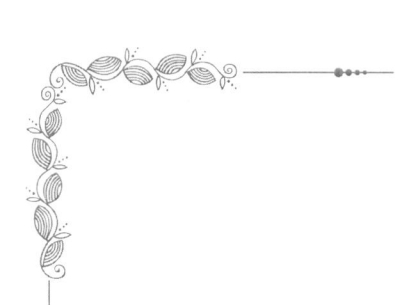

I suppose I've just got to let him go;
let him have space to be - a horse,
for a while. Well, I thought, what else?
We are talking horse for real,
or something aren't we?

Anyway, he came to stay,
and she came too… often,
and he played her up like anything;
I watched from my window;
he wanted out, really.

He had an issue now and again;
I witnessed it. One day it snowed, and she
wasn't there. He loved it and galloped
like Pegasus eight times round the field,
mane flying; not an Issue to be seen.

They took him away in a horse-box
that day to protect him from
the enjoyment of his choice;
life without Mother.
I know who has an issue, and it isn't Pegasus.

Sun's captive

The sun strode in one morning,
my quiet door was shut;
He threw his cloak upon the chair.
Such arrogance was that.

I did not glance to chide him;
my wheel whirled as I bid.
The Lord Sun kissed my fingers
but I no greeting gave.

He burnished in the copper
pots and pans upon my shelf.
He crept in every corner
but could not reach myself.

I heard a happy music
and then he caught my eye.
We ran together up the stair
my friend the sun and I.

The little one was waking.
Remember if you can;
did you wake up one morning
and smile to see the sun?

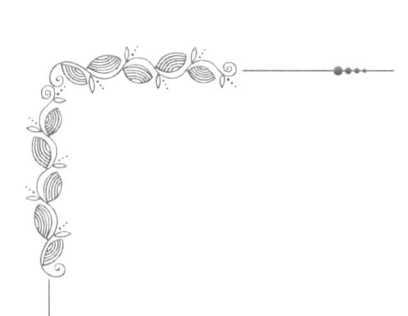

The Door

They always come back to that
painting of Jesus holding a lantern
and knocking at a closed door,
as if it were completely new to us.
I mean, the fact that there is no handle
to open it from His side.

Well we've got the idea; the handle is
on our side for turning, if we want to, so
that He can come in. Yes, Mr Holman Hunt,
you got it right, straight from the book.
And in He comes, smiling, and we have supper
together. That is a happy ending.

In my topsy-turvy world, I'm outside
the door, on my knees waiting for just
a glimpse through a slit, of a new dimension
when He opens it. I swear I can hear Him
moving about, singing, making ready, together
with the Other Two for our banquet forever.

Storming Heaven

Let us pray:
let us storm Heaven now,
as we cry still for those
hacked to pieces, butchered in Syria.
We know this is true;
we have been told by an anguished onlooker
who heard their screams.
Perhaps God heard their pleas for the souls
of their murderers, like St. Stephen.
We weep still for the invisible; the special children,
orphans; those innocents,
hungry, cold, numb; standing in the rubble
that was home; the mothers, inconsolable.

But are we grieving perhaps
for the victims, the captives who stand already
before the throne, washed in the blood
of the Lamb
in their spotless robes, holding high their
palms of martyrdom?
Are they safe now in the everlasting Joy
of the Holy Ghost?
O all those friends for whom we pray,
if you have brushed past
the parted wings of the Angels
and stand now before the throne singing
the heavenly Liturgy, remember us.
KYRIE ELEISON, CHRISTE ELEISON, KYRIE ELEISON.

Pray for us
for our part in this Holocaust;
for our share in the profits of those who
take care that we retain our comfortable lives.
Let us pray and never cease to pray for
Peace in our time. Amen.

SONNETS

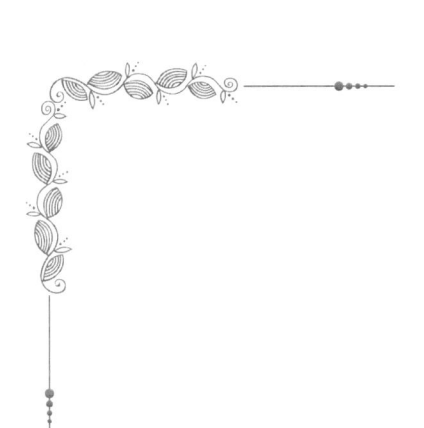

Beauty Risen

All this young April, chaffinch with your note
You strew such wanton memories of song,
I hear another April in your throat
Another Spring in which we shall belong.
For buds and briers begotten of the Fall
Live on, and all their prescient duty is
For this, a pregnant beauty to recall
The coming and the climax of our bliss.
O pity me you violets with your truth,
Whose colour sorrow wears, whose scent is green
With presage of all beauty and all truth
Remind me that such love was never seen.

        For here upon this Rood our Saviour towers
        Deep roots in Eden, but in Heaven he flowers.

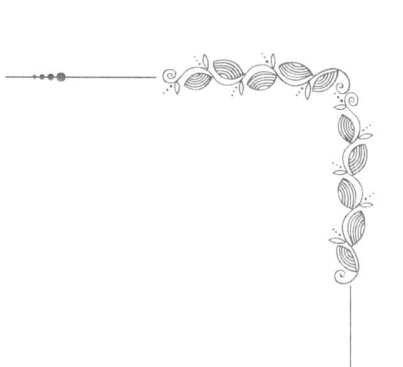

Lachrymae Rerum

For all this beauty too much sadness won
Weeps all in gilded tears over the bay.
Tears of things laced in the netted sun
Sapphire to king's royal lapping away
Into pale, frail, birdshell blue.
And the pearl and feel nearly of water
Sounds and rounds us, eddies us up to you,
Our world's steerer, the wild sea's Master.
Not only cormorant and gull glory and glide
Though, hover and dive the waves under,
Our eyes lustre or heart's hurt
Heal, quite caught in this world's wonder.

   King, tender of birdsong and trees
   What God but you weds to such earth such seas.

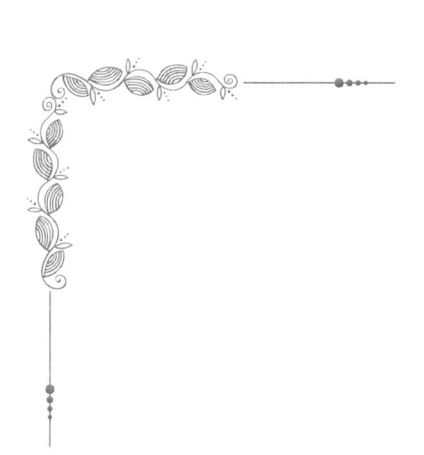

Terra Incognita

I found a flower in bloom, so blue so fair
That promised what I'd long been searching for.
A name it had particular and rare,
A godly, wise and holy gift it bore.
I cradled it, my song one long, sweet note,
Not yet a triad for a chord complete,
But silence healed my parched and thirsting throat,
And I found quiet waiting still more sweet.
I gazed within the flower's trellised heart
Hedged round with petals bright as jewelled crown.
Its secret by the lattice kept apart,
In caverns deep, its mysteries unknown

      I blissful knew we shall be like to God
      When lured by love to terrain yet untrod.

Sonnet for Jean Leclercq

There came a Jester clowning at earth's door
Brains frown in tragedy: pace the floor;
Muddy the beautiful water of worlds, deplore
The glory that fades, foretell angst evermore.
Joie de vivre came, we brought him wine
He laughed and danced for joy of the sun and rain.
We met a fool, whose folly was wisdom's gain.
And excited as swallows arrowed towards the sun
Bellying in the far, blue deeps of the wild,
The highways of the sky, we were beguiled
By the bright distillation, his wonder a child
Feels to shake the kaleidoscope of life

        And make his brilliant pattern. To love, to stake
        All for heaven. A Jester for Jesus' sake.

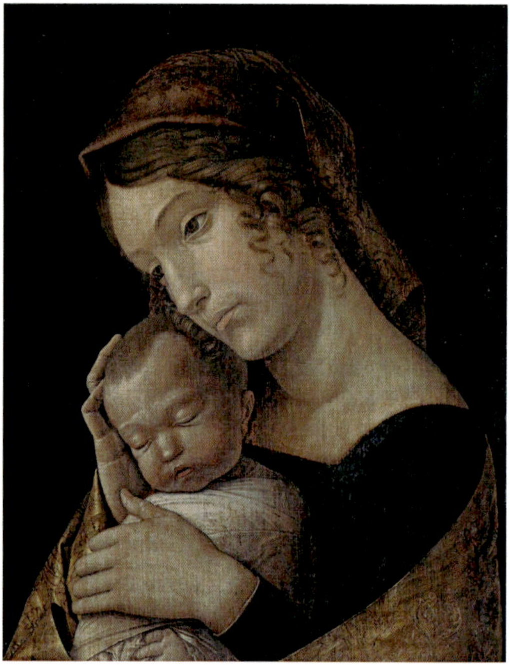

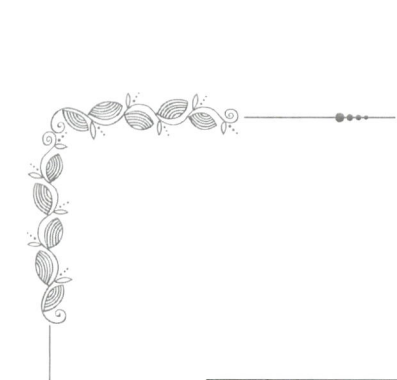

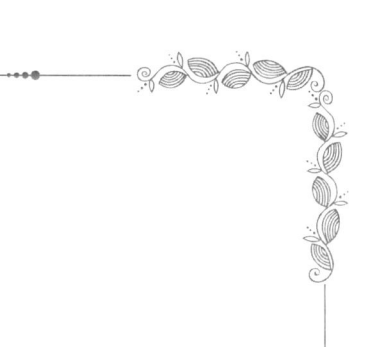

On "The Mother with the sleeping Child"

This mother is remote from me. What does
She see? Those eyes hold too much pain for us,
Those tranquil eyes that agonise, that search
Such depths we scarce can bear ourselves to reach,
 Beseech, or more compel to enter there
And one with her all grieving be our care.
This maid's eyes know no man but only one
So helpless on her breast, this little son
His warm head sidled to her hand. "O come,"
She says, "My love, come back into my womb,
For cradled there what man can give you pain?
My beating heart shall rock you yet again."

    If tender is this blissful motherhood
    How safe shall we be, mothered in our God!

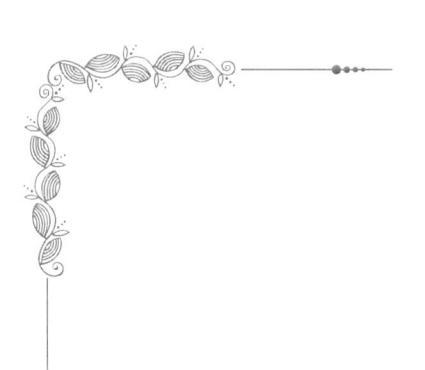

On hearing Bach's B Minor Prelude and Fugue

Abandon us to feel for what you are?
Your glory thunders Lord, then fails our ear.
The ecstatic chord your world invades so far,
Shall silence more your true impression bear?
We are imprisoned in a skein of sound,
The disparate melodic ends to find,
To hold, resolve and finally resound
Complete, refined in counterpoint confined.
But partially your form in music's found,
The master's Prelude to eternity
Our ear yet muted, hears the Fugue that crowned
The search of Bach's immortal clarity.

    But when at last we see your beauty risen,
    Then ear, eye, mind and heart complete the vision.

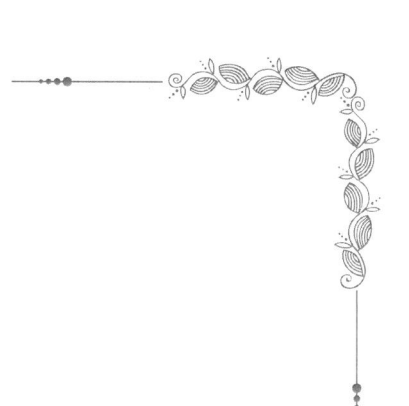

Trinity

Myself a child, a theorem learned by rote
Three sides and angles equal each to each,
What name it answered to, what length to note
Why thus far and no more its lines should reach.
The mind engaged, my heart was loath to trust
Such figure proffered when my God I sought,
Nor trefoil clover, destined soon for dust,
A heartfelt answer to my questing brought.
Then from a burning Word my soul caught flame
The Father's image branded on His Son
With fiery cross upheld, the Spirit came;
Down-bearing, aweful, threefold Holy one.

> I wept that God bore wounded hands for me
> And bade me bear such weight of Trinity.

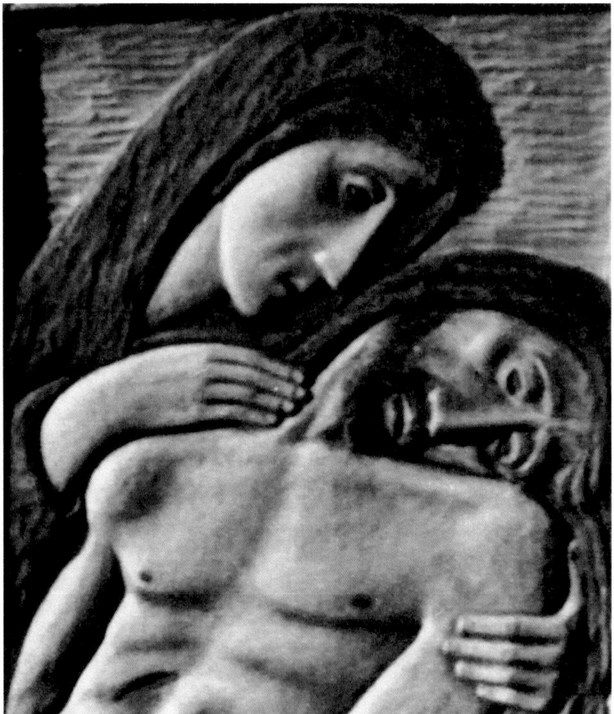

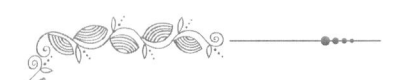

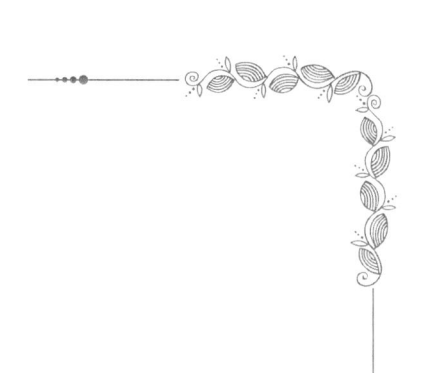

Pietà

The dead remember not the earliest things,
Nor unformed body quick within the womb
But I mind sound of mighty angel's wings
As now I hear men's tread towards the tomb.
I then contained you, sudden and confused
Espoused the eager, outstretched quest of God,
And I remember terror unrefused
And I remember joy past telling of.
Your young glance met mine, quiet as a dove
To make all heaven with trembling earth combine,
Thus thrust into the living flame of love
By grace imprinted from that gaze divine.

    At last those same eyes see the Father's face
    While closed to mine, so dead in my embrace.

EPILOGUE
Part 1

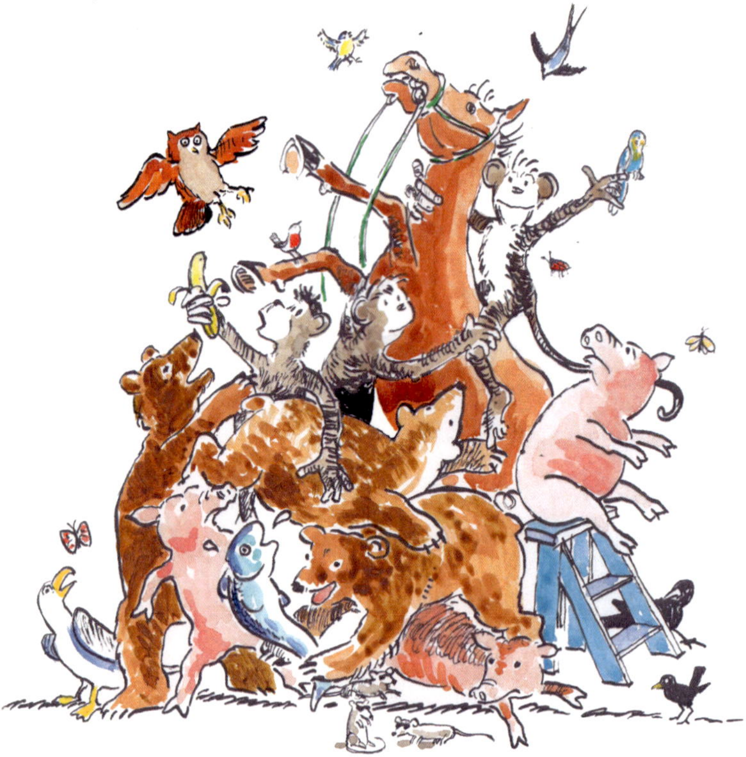

I wonder if you noticed
(I had not realised)
so many creatures were shoving
and elbowing their way
through my poems.
Such a noisy crowd; growling
squeaking, baying, hooting,
threesomes, arm in arm
fish gawping through the ice;
horses getting the better
of folks like us,
not forgetting poor budgie
in his sorrow
in the middle of the rabble.
And then the owl, ladybird,
chaffinch, robin, blackbird,
when will it end, this queue
of rowdy interlopers
traipsing, dancing through
the silence and calm landscape
of my thoughts and all my
heavenly serenity?
"Let us in," they shout
in chorus "we want to be
in your Epilogue."
O such a melange
of insubordination!

EPILOGUE
Part 2

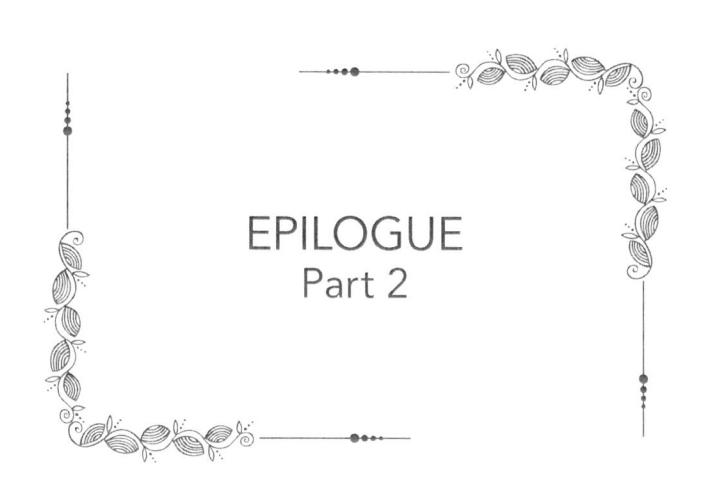

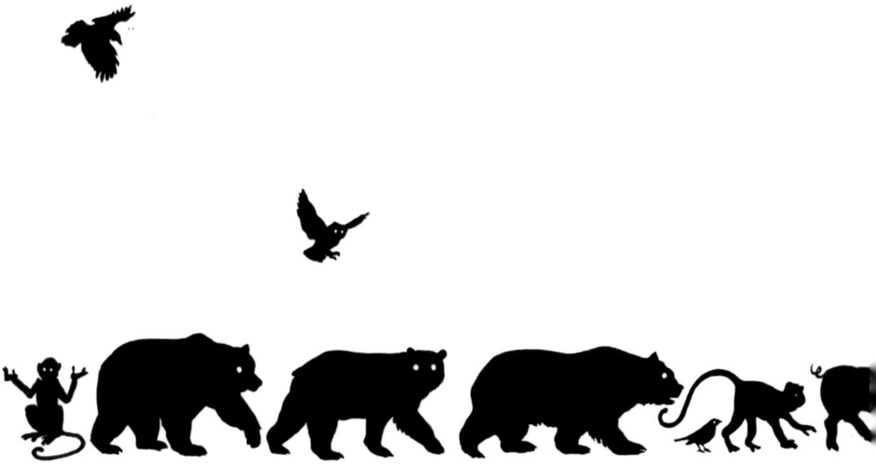

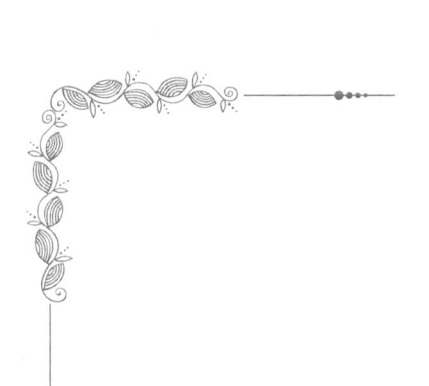

Ah well, open this last page
then; let them come in, holding
paws, claws, hooves, to dance a
fandango out of the last
paragraph of my book.
Life is, after all a celebration
of the diversity of creation;
of bounteous beatitude; the very
laughter of God, as He rejoices eternally in
his creatures, and we all go out together
into the utterly strange and awesome truth;
His overwhelming love, for just as He breathed
out the birth of the world, with Aleph
now at the end, He breathes His last,
with the thunderous 'Tetelestai' of
final consummation resounding through
the black tunnel of death and transposed into
a fanfare of Resurrection echoing over the
golden horizon leading onto the pastures of Eternity